Cavaliers &
Roundheads

The Story of the Civil War with
Stand-up Scenes

Bob Moulder

Tarquin Publications

Bob Moulder was born in London in 1954 and studied art in Belfast. After some years in Salisbury, he now lives in Derby and works as a freelance illustrator. His previous books include 'The French Revolution for Beginners' and 'Western Wonders' which gives an account of the battles of Lansdown and Roundway Down in graphic novel format. These two linked battles were of great importance in the story of the Civil War and are featured on pages 24 & 25 in this book. He is at present working on a graphic novel history of the Italian Renaissance.

©1997: Bob Moulder
I.S.B.N.: 1 8996 18 02 3
Editors: Alan and Sue Metters
Design: Magdalen Bear
Printing: Ancient House Press, Ipswich

CE

All rights reserved

Tarquin Publications
Stradbroke
Diss
Norfolk IP21 5JP
England

The Story of the English Civil War

The Storming of Basing House

1625:	Charles 1 Comes to the Throne	4
	Scene 1: The Period of 'Personal Rule'	7
1637:	A Court Wedding	8
	Troubled Kingdoms	10
1638:	The Ordeal of John Lilburne	11
	The Short & Long Parliaments	12
	Cavaliers & Roundheads	13
1642:	"All My Birds Have Flown"	14
	People Begin to Take Sides	16
	Scene 2: A 'State of War' is Declared	19
	The Battle of Edgehill	20
	Troopers & Tactics	22
1643:	The Battles of Lansdown & Roundway Down	24
	Desperate Times for Parliament	26
1644:	Scene 3: Newark is Besieged	29
	The Battle of Marston Moor	30
	Frustration Sets in	32
1645:	The Battle of Naseby	33
1646:	The War Comes to an End	34
1648:	Negotiations Fail and War is Resumed	36
1649:	Charles is Brought to Trial	37
	Scene 4: The Execution	41
1649:	The Commonwealth is Established	42
1653:	The Protectorate	43
1660:	The Restoration of the Monarchy	44

1625: Charles 1 Comes to the Throne

Charles was twenty five years old when he came to the throne. He was small in stature, reserved and haughty, but always dignified. He had only become the heir to the throne in 1612, as a consequence of the death of his tall and impressive elder brother Henry.

Charles I became King of England and Scotland on March 27, 1625, following the death of his father, James I. England and Scotland were then separate, independent countries but Charles was the King of both. He also claimed to rule all of Ireland but not all Irishmen agreed with him.

The first four years of the new reign were to prove both turbulent and unhappy. Charles kept as his chief adviser his father's favourite, George Villiers, the Duke of Buckingham. This became increasingly unacceptable to many of his leading subjects including some Members of Parliament. They felt that Buckingham had too much power and he was loudly criticised for his expensive failures in wars against Spain and France. They neither liked the King's demands for extra money nor Buckingham's support for a religious policy which seemed to be moving Protestant England closer to Roman Catholicism. At this time the law said that everyone had to attend services in the Protestant Church of England and, as today, the monarch was the head of the established church. Roman Catholics were seen by Charles's Protestant subjects (especially the most extreme, the Puritans) as dangerous traitors.

Charles consistently defended Buckingham against the criticisms of the MP's in the three Parliaments which met in 1625, 1626 and 1628. By 1628, handbills were being passed around in London saying "Who rules the kingdom? The King. Who rules the King? The Duke. Who rules the Duke? The Devil." The King was also hurt and angered when both MP's and the common people rejoiced to hear that Buckingham had been stabbed to death at Portsmouth by a former soldier, John Felton. Less than a year later, in 1629, after more criticism by MP's of royal financial and religious policies, Charles decided to rule without a Parliament. Eleven years of 'Personal Rule' followed, with the King governing from The Royal Court. Here he was happy. He loved his French Catholic wife, Henrietta Maria, and increasingly turned to her for advice. He did not appear to notice the growing discontent of his subjects.

It is important to remember that the seventeenth-century Parliament was very different from its modern equivalent. There were two houses, the Lords and the Commons, as today, but the monarch alone could decide when Parliament should be called or dissolved. Most people could not vote, this right being restricted to men of property and the best way to become an MP was to find an influential patron or sponsor. Nevertheless, many historians argue that Parliament had already become an important part of the government and it was sensible for a monarch to consult his leading subjects in this way, particularly when new laws were needed or new taxes had to be raised.

Scene 1: The Period of 'Personal Rule'

The Court was the centre of government and the King was its heart. Charles I was a firm believer in the Divine Right of Kings. He viewed himself as God's chosen representative and any opposition to him was effectively opposition to God.

He felt that he had really tried to rule in collaboration with Parliament but his MP's had proved too turbulent and disobedient. He thought that it would be far better for these critical and troublesome subjects to return to their estates while he ruled his realm from his Court. Here he could be content with his wife, enjoy his growing family and continue to add to his collection of paintings.

During the 1630's in London it was not unusual to look out across the river Thames and see a stately procession of large, richly adorned rowing boats making their way down river from the Palace of Whitehall.

Following the bend of the river at Charing Cross, they would pass the Inns of Court, then Henry VIII's old Palace of Bridewell to reach the point where the river Fleet joined the Thames. Here the helmsmen would manoeuvre their craft towards a jetty attached to a large town house, close by the forbidding looking bulk of Baynard's Castle. Liveried boatmen would secure the boats and halberdiers would take post.

The cut-out pieces for this scene are on page 45. The instructions on how to assemble it are inside the back cover.

This area glues to page 7

The Period of 'Personal Rule'

How to assemble Scene 1
1. Remove page 5 from the book by cutting along the solid line.
2. Cut out the T-shaped piece precisely.
3. Score along the dotted line, creasing firmly to make a valley fold.
4. Check how the grey area on the back of the text fits over this grey area so that the flap forms the backdrop of the scene. Then glue it carefully into position.

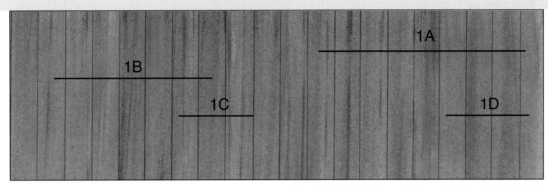

King Charles had come to have his portrait painted by the great Flemish artist Anthony Van Dyck, 'Principal Painter in Ordinary to their Majesties'. This house in Blackfriars was his residence and his studio.

Van Dyck spent several years in England and the numerous portraits he produced bring the Court of Charles I vividly to life. In fact the large painting shown here now hangs in the National Gallery. The 'three face' portrait is in the Royal Collection at Windsor Castle.

Charles was a great patron of the arts, commissioning paintings from not only Van Dyck and the other great Flemish artist Peter Paul Rubens but also from other lesser figures. From the great architect Inigo Jones he commissioned elegant new buildings in the classical style which was so popular in Europe at the time. He also supported and encouraged new developments in science and technology.

1637: A Court Wedding

On August 3, 1637 James Stuart, Duke of Lennox, married Lady Mary Villiers. The King and Queen were delighted by the match, as they were very fond of the couple. Lennox was Charles's cousin, while Lady Mary, lady-in-waiting to the Queen, was the daughter of the late Duke of Buckingham. The Archbishop of Canterbury, William Laud, conducted the service at Lambeth Palace and the King gave the bride away. The reception afterwards was a marvellously happy occasion for the Court, marred only by a thunderstorm that sent the guests scurrying indoors from the gardens.

There would not be many more such happy occasions for the Court of King Charles. Storm clouds were gathering across the whole of Charles's realm and reports arrived daily of unrest in Scotland. Nobody, of course, could know that this would lead eventually to civil war; or that the war would claim the lives of all three of the groom's brothers, George, John and Bernard. Other wedding guests, such as the Earl of Denbigh, would also die in battle; while Archbishop Laud, the Duke of Hamilton and eventually Charles himself would be executed.

All of the people illustrated here were painted at least once by Van Dyck. Some can be seen in the National Gallery or the National Portrait Gallery in London or in the Royal Collection at Windsor Castle. Ignoring the musicians and other onlookers the guests from left to right were:
James Hamilton, Duke of Hamilton
William Feilding, 1st Earl of Denbigh
Susan Villiers, Countess of Denbigh.

Beyond the urn:
Lord George Stuart, Seigneur d'Aubigny
Lord John Stuart
Charles Hamilton, Earl of Arran
Lord Bernard Stuart.

The bride and groom:
Lady Mary Villiers, Duchess of Lennox
James Stuart, 4th Duke of Lennox.

On the groom's left:
Princess Mary
Catherine Manners, Duchess of Buckingham
Charles, Prince of Wales
King Charles I
Queen Henrietta Maria
Lucy Percy, Countess of Carlisle.

Troubled Kingdoms

While the King was enjoying his family and courtly life many of his subjects in England and Scotland were much less happy. The disputes about religion and money matters continued.

Religion

The Puritans in England wanted plain churches, simple services and much preaching to pass on the Word of God. Archbishop Laud was determined to reform the Church of England and to make the services more ceremonial. He wanted the churches themselves to be more beautiful and to be decorated for the glory of God. There was a great dispute over whether the communion service should take place sitting round a communion table in the centre of the church, as the Puritans wanted, or kneeling at an altar in the east end of the church, as Archbishop Laud ordered.

Each side thought that it was right and that the other side was dangerously wrong. Laud was even prepared to put in the pillory such Puritans as William Prynne, Henry Burton and John Bastwick, who preached against the power of bishops and against the life of the Court. The Puritans believed that Laud was trying to make England Roman Catholic again. They were wrong but it did not help that throughout the 1630's messengers from the Pope in Rome were cordially received at Court.

Money

While many of Charles's subjects were increasingly unhappy about his religious policies, his financial policies had become equally unpopular. Without Parliament to raise money for him, Charles resorted to schemes which, although legal, aroused great hostility. He compelled all men who owned property worth £40 a year either to become knights and to pay fees for the privilege or pay a heavy fine. He also fined those landowners who had used lands in royal forests during past centuries. And, most importantly, he extended the collection of 'Ship Money'. This was a traditional way of raising money in coastal areas for ship-building during time of war. Charles extended Ship Money to the whole country when England was not at war and this provoked great resentment. One Puritan squire, John Hampden, decided to oppose the levy in the law courts. The case dragged on for a year until, in April 1638, a majority of the judges decided in favour of the King. Charles had won, but only by a very narrow margin and Hampden appeared to many to be the real hero in the affair. However, at the same time as these matters were unfolding in England, events in Scotland were becoming of even greater concern to the King.

Scotland and the First Bishops' War

In 1636 Charles I had ordered the Scots to use the English prayer book. He failed to seek the approval of either the Scottish Parliament or the Kirk as the Presbyterian Church was known. The Scottish Presbyterians had similar beliefs to those of the English Puritans and they were determined to resist both the prayer book and Charles's desire to rule the Scottish Church through the appointment of bishops.

The new Prayer Book was introduced throughout Scotland in July 1637. In St. Giles Cathedral, in Edinburgh, when the Dean, Dr. Hannah, began one particular service a pre-arranged riot started. A woman named Jenny Geddes shouted "The mass is come among us" and hurled a stool at the Dean. Books and other stools soon followed and the riot continued even after the protesters had been ejected. Similar demonstrations took place at other churches throughout Scotland.

To Charles this was rebellion and he was determined to enforce his authority. Those members of the clergy who obeyed him faced noisy disobedience, although some, like the Bishop of Brechin, were prepared to lead religious services with a pair of pistols close at hand. In February and March 1638 Presbyterian Scots of all classes flocked to sign 'The Covenant', a vow to defend the true faith of Scotland against all English innovations. By early 1639 they were praying, preaching and also drilling in arms under their general, Alexander Leslie. Victory went to the Scots in this first 'Bishops' War' of 1639, although there was little real fighting. The King was humiliated, both because his own army was seen to be very badly equipped and also because he had no money. He agreed to a truce and then summoned the first English Parliament for eleven years. Many English Puritans sympathised with the Scots.

1638: The Ordeal of John Lilburne

The crowd could hear the tap-tap of the drum and the crack of the whip. The young man could be seen staggering along behind a cart, the three-pronged whip falling every three or four paces as he made his painful journey from the Fleet Prison to the pillory in Old Palace Yard, Westminster.

The crowd spoke words of comfort and murmured their disapproval. Priests and agents of the Pope now moved openly at Court, it was said, while a good Puritan like this John Lilburne was hauled before the Court of Star Chamber and then whipped through the streets like a dog. And for what? Because he sought to distribute the Puritan Bastwick's book 'Letany' which condemned bishops as enemies of God.

The crowd marvelled at the spirit of Lilburne. Breathless though he was, they could hear him reciting the scriptures and denouncing the bishops. Soon he had so agitated the crowd that an official came with an offer to lessen his sentence if he would remain silent. He refused and stoically saw out his punishment in the pillory.

England had not heard the last of 'Freeborn John', as he came to be nicknamed. After fighting for Parliament in the First Civil War he became a leading 'Leveller', seeking to build a more just society out of all the bloodshed and the suffering.

The Short & Long Parliaments

The Short Parliament

The new Parliament met on April 13, 1640 and all the resentments of the past eleven years of 'Personal Rule' erupted. Under the leadership of John Pym, a Puritan with legal experience and nicknamed 'Ox' by the Court, the House of Commons refused to grant Charles any money until their grievances had been considered. After three weeks the King, in frustration, dissolved the 'Short Parliament', as it became known. But the King's other problems were not so easily dissolved.

The Long Parliament

A second Bishops' War followed and was even more disastrous for the King. The Scots crossed the border and occupied Newcastle, one of England's leading ports. Charles was now forced to agree to pay their army a large sum of money each month and, in even more humiliating circumstances, he once again summoned Parliament. This Parliament is now known as the 'Long Parliament' because it did not officially dissolve itself for twenty years. However, in fact it only met from November 1640 until December 1648, the date when its more moderate members were excluded in order to prepare for the trial of the King.

Root and Branch

Between the autumn of 1640 and the summer of 1641 the Long Parliament destroyed the most unpopular parts of the King's financial policy, including Ship Money, and also hated law courts like the Court of Star Chamber. Archbishop Laud was condemned for his religious policy and imprisoned in the Tower of London. Charles's other chief adviser, the Earl of Strafford, was tried on a trumped-up charge of treason and condemned to death. Parliament's supporters rejoiced when 'Black Tom Tyrant' as Strafford had become known was beheaded on Tower Hill on May 12, 1641. Charles had signed the death warrant reluctantly, only to protect his Catholic Queen who was also hated by the Puritan Londoners. Everything seemed to be against the King; he even had to agree to call Parliament at least every three years and not to dissolve it without its own consent.

Yet by autumn 1641 it was clear that many moderate MP's felt that enough reforms had already been agreed. They did not want further attacks on the leaders of society and the Church, and they opposed a bill to remove bishops from the House of Lords. The moderates feared that the kind of Puritan who wanted to destroy the system of bishops with the 'Root and Branch' petition would also want to attack the privileges of the aristocracy and gentry. A Royalist party was beginning to emerge even within Parliament itself.

The Grand Remonstrance

In November 1641, Pym attempted to rally support and introduced the 'Grand Remonstrance', a list of Parliament's grievances against the King's government. However when it came to the vote, he found that he had over-estimated his own strength and had a majority of only eleven. The bill was passed by 159 votes to 148.

Clearly there were now two sides in the conflict.

Cavaliers & Roundheads

The divisions grew wider. On November 25, the King returned to London after negotiating with the Scots and was cheered by the London crowds. Believing that he now had popular support, he was determined to re-assert his control. However, English Protestants were still shuddering at stories of atrocities in Northern Ireland where Irish Catholics had rebelled violently against the Protestant settlers. London apprentices now wandered about the streets shouting "No bishops! No popery!"

In December Charles appointed Thomas Lunsford, an ardent Royalist with an unsavoury reputation, to the position of Governor of the Tower of London, the capital's chief weapons store. On the 28th the Londoners demonstrated their feelings. Chanting "No bishops!" and "Butcher Lunsford out!", a large crowd of plainly dressed young men, traders and apprentices from the city, moved down Whitehall, past the clock tower and into Old Palace Yard. Here they harangued people entering the Palace of Westminster. Some even forced their way into the Great Hall where the courts of the King's Bench and Chancery were trying to conduct business.

John Williams, Archbishop of York, arriving to take his seat in the Lords, was incensed by the tumult. In a most unholy manner, he leapt from his coach to assail one lad who was yelling abuse against the bishops. He soon had to be rescued from the fists of the furious apprentices.

Barely had this fracas died down when another occurred in the Great Hall itself. Here the apprentices found Thomas Lunsford and a number of other 'gentlemen' strutting about like peacocks. The apprentices decided that they were not true English gentlemen but more like the rowdy, cut-throat, papist knights their preachers had warned them of. They were more like Spanish 'caballeros' or Italian 'cavalieri', the more learned suggested. Less educated tongues preferred to call them 'Cavaliers'.

Lunsford's group soon tired of the taunting. Captain David Hyde threatened to "Cut the throats of these round-headed dogs who bawl against the bishops." The term round-headed for these insolent, crop-haired apprentices became 'Roundheads', and began to be used for any supporter of the Parliamentary side. Lunsford drew his sword, scattering the apprentices. They gave chase but out in Old Palace Yard were met by a hail of stones. The guard was called out but could not disperse the crowd until Lunsford himself left the scene. The apprentices demonstrated again on the next two days, which saw even worse violence. John Lilburne was in the thick of it and was wounded leading an attempted breakout of gaoled demonstrators. As the Christmas holiday drew to a close, the city returned to an uneasy calm.

Thomas Lunsford and other gentlemen in a fracas with rioting apprentices in the Old Palace Yard at Westminster. It was almost certainly from this encounter that the terms 'Roundheads' and 'Cavaliers' came to be used for the two sides in the Civil War.

1642: "All My Birds Have Flown"

On January 4, 1642 the King made a crucial mistake. At three o'clock in the afternoon, word reached the House of Commons that Charles was on his way personally with an armed guard to arrest six Parliamentary leaders: John Pym, John Hampden and three other members of the Commons together with Lord Kimbolton from the Lords. The previous day, charges had been read out in the Lords accusing the six of high treason. Extraordinarily, no immediate attempt was made to arrest them and the element of surprise was lost. When eventually Charles demanded that Parliament surrender the men, both the Lords and the Commons refused. Spurred on by the Queen, he now came to strike the blow that would restore his authority.

But, forewarned, the six members were excused by their colleagues and slipped away by boat to the City of London as the King entered the Great Hall. While his armed retinue waited outside, Charles, accompanied by his nephew the Elector Palatine (the exiled ruler of a German state), entered the Commons. The members rose and stood in aggrieved silence. No King had ever come uninvited into this chamber. The privilege of Parliament had been abused.

Calmly Charles crossed the floor and asked the Speaker, William Lenthall, if he might borrow his chair. He then addressed the house. "Gentlemen, I am sorry for this occasion, yet you must know that in cases of treason, no person hath a privilege. Therefore I am come to know if any of these persons that were accused are here." He scanned the rows of MP's. "Is Mr. Pym here?" On receiving no answer, he asked the Speaker if any of the accused were present. "Sire," replied the Speaker, "I have neither eyes to see nor tongue to speak in this place but as the House is pleased to direct me." The King surveyed the sea of faces. "Hum ... 'tis no matter ... I think my eyes are as good as another's." The awful silence continued until Charles, in resignation, added "Since I see all my birds have flown, I do expect that you will send them unto me as soon as they return hither."

The Parliamentary leaders had taken their refuge in the City but when Charles went there to demand their surrender, he was greeted with shouts of "Privilege! Privilege!" On January 11, Pym and his colleagues were cheered on their way back to Westminster. The day before that, Charles had taken his family to Hampton Court. They moved on to Windsor and then separated. Henrietta Maria went to Holland to seek help and to try to pawn some of the crown jewels and Charles travelled to Yorkshire to recruit military support. Before parting, they arranged to write to each other in code.

Charles had made a fateful decision in leaving his capital, and England had taken a step nearer to civil war.

The King enters the House of Commons to arrest the six Members of Parliament he accused of high treason.

People Begin to Take Sides

Ten chaotic months were to pass until the first major battle between the Cavaliers and Roundheads. Though King and Parliament continued to negotiate, neither side seemed set on finding a genuine reconciliation.

Having lost London, Charles's first move was to try to secure other key points in the kingdom: major towns, ports and fortresses. He had only limited success with this strategy. He gained the port of Newcastle and for a time Portsmouth but Parliament took control of most of the major ports and, more importantly, the navy.

At that time, there was no regular professional army in England, but Parliament passed a new law without the King's consent called the 'Militia Ordinance'. This placed the county militias, or 'Trained Bands' as they were also known, under Parliamentary control. Charles countered this by issuing 'Commissions of Array' instructing local magistrates to seize county arsenals and to raise troops for a royal army. Both sides knew that the poorly trained and poorly equipped part-time soldiers of the militias would be of only limited use. The really desperate need was to find professional soldiers who could train raw recruits and lead them into battle. Initially therefore both sides modelled their forces on the European armies still engaged in the Thirty Years War. England was not directly involved in this war but numerous Englishmen, mainly from the gentry, had gone to fight for the Protestant cause on the Continent. It was to these men that both sides turned as they attempted to turn their raw recruits into disciplined armies.

Officers were invariably drawn from the gentry and, particularly on the Parliamentary side, the more wealthy middle-classes. Only later did able men of very humble origin become officers. While social rank played a part in the appointment of commanders neither side could afford to ignore genuine ability. The Royalist army in the west country, for instance, was nominally commanded by the Marquis of Hertford and Prince Maurice, but on campaign the more experienced and capable Sir Ralph Hopton, a mere country squire, was the army's actual commander in the field.

Across the country, families were having to take sides and this was not an easy matter. Many did not want to choose. "Oh sweet heart, I am now in a great strait what to do," Thomas Knyvett wrote to his wife in Norfolk from Westminster on May 18. The most activist supporters on both sides tried to persuade others to follow their lead and to give money, horses and men to their cause. Yet most communities were split and, tragically, so were some families. Even the King's own standard-bearer at the first great battle at Edghill was to have one of his sons fighting for Parliament.

The events in Nottingham in the summer of 1642 give some idea of what was happening all over the country.

One day John Hutchinson, the son of the local MP, travelled into Nottingham from his country home to visit the mayor. The mayor was not at home, his wife explained. Sir John Digby, the high sheriff of the county, and Lord Newark, the lord lieutenant, had come to requisition the county's gunpowder supply in the name of the King and the mayor had gone to alert members of the Trained Band.

This news alarmed Hutchinson, for he, like many in that area, was a Puritan and sympathetic to Parliament. Hurrying along to the Town Hall to try to stop or delay the two officials, he found the powder already being weighed out. He approached Lord Newark, a man with a fiery temper, and as tactfully and politely as he could, asked what he intended to do with the powder. "The King having great necessities, desires to borrow it, Mr. Hutchinson," he replied, though he could produce no letter of authority from the King.

"This is satisfactory to me, my Lord, but the county would not be willing to part with its powder in so dangerous a time without an absolute authority." And Hutchinson talked of desperate armed men roving the countryside. Newark was disconcerted by this diplomatic way of telling him to put the powder back. He talked airily of returning it in ten days and was still trying to justify himself when a crowd of angry militia-men turned up. Newark tried to bluster his way out. "The King's occasions are urgent and must be served," he shouted. But eventually he conceded defeat and made to leave.

"I am sorry to find you at the head of this faction, Mr. Hutchinson," Newark angrily remarked as he left with Sir John Digby. "My lord, I came only to prevent mischief and danger that I saw likely to ensue." But by now, Newark could see through the diplomatic niceties. He said that he would inform the King personally of Hutchinson's mischief. "My Lord, I am glad that if the King is to receive information on me it is from so honourable a person," was Hutchinson's final flourish to send the seething Lord Newark on his way.

Hutchinson's efforts in denying the weapons to the King were, however, to be all in vain. It had begun to seem to the King that this verbal sparring would last for ever and that he needed to exert his authority and to bring the stalemate to a rapid end. He therefore asked his dashing nephew Prince Rupert of the Rhine to meet him in Nottingham and to take command of the royal cavalry.

The Prince was then 23 years old and already an experienced commander having fought in many campaigns on the Continent. Hutchinson, hearing of the new determination and a rumour that he was to be arrested, left to join the Parliamentary army at Northampton.

In mid-August the King advanced from York with his small army, to reach Nottingham himself. His hopes that the East Midlands might provide him with the recruits he needed to support his cause were soon dashed. While not openly hostile, the people of Nottingham remained defiantly unsympathetic to the royal cause. At this stage the locks on the magazine doors were broken and the Royalists helped themselves to the powder and weapons.

They were needed. The King had chosen Nottingham as the place for a formal declaration of a state of war. The talking would have to end and the fighting begin.

The cut-out pieces for this scene are on page 45. The instructions on how to assemble it are inside the back cover.

2D

This area glues to page 19

1642: A 'State of War' is Declared

How to assemble Scene 2
1. Remove page 17 from the book by cutting along the solid line.
2. Cut out the T-shaped piece precisely.
3. Score along the dotted line, creasing firmly to make a valley fold.
4. Check how the grey area on the back of the text fits over this grey area so that the flap forms the backdrop of the scene.
   Then glue it carefully into position.

The ceremony of raising the royal standard on August 22, 1642 was the formal declaration that a state of war existed in the Realm. It symbolised that all those who took up arms against the King were traitors and could be brought to trial and hanged.

It took place on Castle Hill on a wet and windy evening. To the sound of drums and trumpets, Charles and his Courtiers watched 'melancholically' as the standard unfurled.

Later that night the standard blew down.

Rupert arrived, but the royal army was still too small to risk confronting the Parliamentary forces. In September Charles left Nottingham for the west and established his base at Shrewsbury. He could then hope to draw on support from Wales, Cheshire and the West Midlands, areas much more sympathetic to the royal cause. This was the case and by the end of September, the King had gathered together an army of 10,000 men.

1642: The Battle of Edgehill

The first major battle at Edgehill near Banbury in Oxfordshire made it clear that the war would not be quickly over.

"Monday morning. I received your letter with my mistress's scarf and Mr. Molloyne's hatband. These gifts I am unworthy of. I shall wear them for your sakes, and I hope I shall never stain them but in the blood of a Cavalier."

So wrote London journeyman, Nehemiah Wharton, now a sergeant in Denzil Holles's regiment of foot, to his old master Mr. Willingham.

On September 23, Prince Rupert, commanding a detachment of the King's Cavaliers, had destroyed a body of Roundhead cavalry at Powicke Bridge near Worcester.

Wharton was not disheartened by the news but wrote further: "They boast wonderfully and swear most hellishly that the next time they meet us they will make but a mouthful of us. But I am persuaded the Lord has given them a small victory, that they may, in the day of battle, come on more presumptuously to their own destruction."

When the Cavalier and Roundhead armies faced each other at Edgehill on October 23, Wharton was to experience the force of Rupert's cavalry at first hand.

The battle opened at 3.00 pm and the Roundhead cavalry on the left flank of Essex's army was immediately swept away by a devastating charge led by Prince Rupert. Just to the rear, Denzil Holles's regiment of foot was thrown into confusion by the wave of fleeing Roundhead cavalry troopers. It was then attacked by the euphoric Cavaliers. There is no record of Wharton's fate but his regiment gave way under this onslaught and Mr. Willingham received no more letters.

The success of the Royalist cavalry should have given the King a rapid victory but Rupert's inexperienced troopers excitedly chased the Roundhead cavalry off the field instead of regrouping to strike a decisive blow at the Roundhead foot. For by now, Essex's infantry was steadily driving the King's infantry back. Fortunes changed when some Roundhead cavalry who had escaped the rout were able to regroup and struck the Royalists a heavy blow in the flank. A defeat for the King began to look more and more certain.

Fighting at the heart of the Royalist foot was Sir Edmund Verney, the bearer of the royal standard. With a casual disregard for death Sir Edmund had declined to wear any armour and placed himself in the thick of it. His bodyguard was killed but Sir Edmund slew two of the enemy before a Roundhead struck him dead and captured the standard.

The King's foot-soldiers did not despair but held on grimly until their cavalry gradually returned. However, by now both armies were too exhausted to continue the fight and the struggle ended with neither side gaining the upper hand.

Though he was heartened to hear that the royal standard had been recaptured, Charles was visibly shaken by the carnage which had taken place; hundreds lay dead or wounded, among them many of his Court. Sixty of his lifeguards lay dead in a heap where the royal standard had been lost. England had not seen fighting like this for over a hundred years.

While Charles hesitated and sorrowed, Essex marched the survivors of the Parliamentary army back from Edgehill to protect London. Prince Rupert followed as far as Brentford but, outnumbered two-to-one, could go no further. Charles then withdrew to Oxford and set up what was to become his headquarters for the duration of the war. It became a garrison town with the colleges of the University offering accommodation and facilities to the royal army. The King lodged at Christ Church and Prince Rupert at St. John's. All Souls' College became an arsenal, New Inn Hall the mint and Merton the treasury. Court life resumed while the King and his advisers tried to devise strategies for regaining control of the kingdom.

It was evident that no speedy conclusion would be reached and both sides settled down to prepare for a long war.

The Cavalier cavalry under the leadership of Prince Rupert launched a devastating charge on the left flank of the Roundheads. Roundhead cavalry fleeing through the Roundhead foot threw everything into confusion and opened them up to attack by the enemy cavalry. However, this initial advantage gained by the King's forces was soon lost and the battle ended with neither side victorious.

Troopers and Tactics

Success in warfare, as always, depended on the balance between offensive and defensive weapons. Cavalry was mostly used to attack but infantry could both attack and defend. A charge of cavalry with thundering horses, slashing swords and exploding pistols might seem impossible for foot soldiers to resist. However, a group armed with pikes which stood firm could inflict terrible damage on horses. A dismounted horseman with his heavy equipment and sword was then very vulnerable. Muskets may have been primitive, but a volley into a mass of advancing horses could scarcely miss and what started as a brave charge could so easily disintegrate into chaos and disaster.

On the other hand, if cavalry could break through the lines, then the infantry could be destroyed at will. Muskets took a very long time to reload and a man with a sword standing on the ground was no match for a galloping horseman. In order to balance the different characteristics, it was found that the most effective proportion for an army was to have one third infantry to two thirds cavalry.

The Cavalry

Two fully equipped Cavalry Troopers

Cavalry regiments varied in size, comprising anything from two to ten squadrons of 50 to 100 men. A well-equipped cavalry trooper had a heavy sword, two pistols and a carbine. In the Thirty Years War cavalry were trained to advance, fire their pistols and then wheel away to reform and reload. Such tactics required a high degree of training.

Prince Rupert realised that it was better to let his raw but exuberant cavalry recruits fire once and then charge home. They did this to devastating effect at Edgehill and it became the standard tactic for the early part of the war. Supporting the cavalry were mounted infantry called dragoons who did not charge but provided covering fire to protect exposed flanks. They could also move cross-country more quickly than infantry and set up ambushes.

The Infantry

An Infantry Officer   **A Musketeer**   **A Pikeman**

A foot regiment in theory comprised about a thousand men. However, casualties, sickness and desertion, not to mention the difficulty of finding recruits, meant that few regiments on either side had even half this number.

The infantry consisted of musketeers and pikemen in the ratio of about two to one. The musketeer was armed with a matchlock musket. This was a cumbersome weapon with an effective range of only 100 metres and a lengthy reloading process but it was much more effective than the bows and arrows which had gone before. Musketeers generally fought in six ranks, each rank firing and then dropping back to reload. Even then, the rate of fire was slow and they needed the protection given by the pikemen with their five metre pikes. Pikemen could also be used to spearhead an assault.

Sieges

The best form of defence was to withdraw inside a substantial fortification and so be protected by stone walls, ditches and moats. It then needed a very much larger army on the outside to defeat a smaller army on the inside. It was most unusual for an attacking force to make a direct assault on a besieged town as the cost in lives was too high. What attackers did was to mount a siege. This would continue until either the walls were breached by gunfire or explosives or the occupants began to starve. It might, and did, take years.

The Civil War saw many sieges; Newark saw three. It commanded the road from London to York and was never captured. It only surrendered when the Royalist cause was lost. Generally towns based their defence upon their old medieval fortifications, and improved them by building extra ramparts of earth in a zig-zag lay-out. The aim was to channel attackers into positions where their exposed flanks could be fired upon. Some of the Civil War fortifications can still be seen in Newark today.

Laying siege to a town was not easy. The besiegers would have to camp in cold muddy fields and be shot at by snipers secure behind embrasures in the walls. They might also be attacked at any time by raiding parties sent out through the gates. After all this, there was always the chance that after months of effort, a well-armed and fresh relieving force would arrive and attack the besiegers from the rear.

If artillery could not breach the walls, the attacking army could try other methods. One was to dig a mine under the wall, place explosives in it and then detonate them. Of course if the defenders got wind of this digging, they might start a counter-mine to attack it. Sometimes there was even hand-to-hand combat underground. A desperate alternative was to use a petard, an explosive device. A volunteer rushed forward with it and tried to embed it in the wall. He ignited the fuse and dashed for cover. If it went off prematurely, the poor volunteer was deemed to have been 'hoist with his own petard'.

Artillery and Guns

Each army had artillery, but in the seventeenth century guns were so heavy as to be of limited use on the battlefield except for defending or attacking a stronghold. Heavy cannons were essential for this purpose and for sieges the most common were the medium heavy pieces; the culverin (6.8kg) and the demi-cannon (12.3kg). Sometimes the enormous cannon-royal with its 28.6kg shot was used. Guns such as these would have required many men and a minimum of eight or nine horses or twice as many oxen to pull them along the muddy unmade roads of the period.

Cannon fire was not very accurate or effective at ranges greater than about 300 metres, although a shot would travel as far as 1000 metres. At longer ranges solid iron cannon balls were used but it was found that at close range case-shot was more effective. This consisted of a canister of musket balls which burst on firing, rather like a modern shotgun cartridge. Mortars using explosive shells might also be used.

The Parliamentary forces relied on artillery pieces manufactured in Kent, Sussex and London, whereas the Royalists, particularly after 1643, tended to use guns imported from abroad or captured from the enemy. Considerable amounts of gunpowder also came from abroad, particularly from the United Provinces of the Netherlands. Powder could also be made locally, however, where the raw materials (sulphur, charcoal and potassium nitrate) were available.

Pistols were fired by a spark produced either by a wheel-lock (with a steel wheel rotating against a piece of pyrite) or a flintlock (where a piece of flint struck against a steel plate). Matchlock muskets were fired in much the same way. They were slow and cumbersome things to reload and so, in close combat, musketeers had to be ready to use their swords or to wield their muskets like a club. This led to the saying 'push of pike and dint of butt' to describe infantry fighting.

A cannon being made ready for firing

1643: The Battles of Lansdown & Roundway Down

With their commander, Sir Bevil Grenville, at their head, the Cornish pikemen made a near suicidal attack uphill. Sir Bevil was killed as they reached the brow of the hill, but they succeeded in dislodging the Roundheads from their strong defensive position.

Gradually the majority of the country became embroiled in the war and strong lines of division began to develop. From his base in Oxford, the King could control much of the West Midlands and Wales and continue to pose a threat to London. The Cavaliers also made substantial gains in the north after the victory of Adwalton Moor in Yorkshire. Although the east and south-east were dominated by Parliamentarians, the King could see an opportunity opening up in the south-west.

At the start of 1643, the situation in the west had not looked promising as Wiltshire, Somerset, Dorset and Devon were all solidly for Parliament. However, Sir Ralph Hopton had managed to secure Cornwall and, after a victory at the Battle of Stratton, overran Devon and advanced boldly into Somerset. The King sent him further reinforcements under the command of the Marquis of Hertford and Prince Maurice, the younger brother of Prince Rupert. He hoped that this strengthened army would be able to take the important port of Bristol and then join him in Oxford for an assault on London. Success in such a plan would finish the war.

To frustrate this plan Parliament sent a Roundhead army under the command of Sir William Waller, an old friend of Sir Ralph Hopton. Only a month earlier, Waller had written to Hopton:

"My affections to you are so unchangeable, that hostility itself cannot violate my friendship to your person. But I must be true to the cause wherein I serve. That great God knows with what sad sense I go upon this service and with what perfect hatred I detest this war without an enemy. We must act those parts that are assigned to us in this tragedy. Let us do so in a way of honour."

The first part of this two-stage confrontation took place on Lansdown Hill, near Bath, on July 5, 1643. Waller's army had set up a strong defensive position on the hill itself and Hopton considered it too strong to risk attacking. However, the Cornish foot were determined they could take it. With their commander Sir Bevil Grenville at their head the pikemen advanced up the steep hill, raked with canon and musket fire every step of the way. Grenville fell at the brow of the hill, but they had succeeded in forcing the Roundheads to retreat.

A desperate Roundhead counter-attack by Sir Arthur Hasilrig and his 'lobsters', as they were called after their extensive body armour, failed to turn the course of the battle. Hasilrig was struck by sword blows and even suffered a point blank shot from a pistol. Yet his armour protected him and he sustained no serious injury. Eventually two Cavaliers compelled him to surrender but he was then freed by another Roundhead charge. Charles later joked, "Had he been victualled as well as fortified he might have endured a siege of seven years."

It was a hollow victory, however. The loss of Grenville was compounded the following day by the accidental explosion of a powder wagon which left Hopton seriously injured. The Royalists then tried to reach Oxford but were too weak and short of arms and powder. They entered Devizes for protection but the Roundheads quickly arrived and Waller was convinced he had the enemy at his mercy. However, he was unable to prevent the Royalist Cavalry from breaking free, so allowing a party led by Prince Maurice to reach Oxford for reinforcements and fresh supplies.

On July 13, having failed to finish off Hopton's army, Waller saw the Royalist relief force approaching from the direction of Oxford. Quickly wheeling his army about, he drew it up on Roundway Down ready to meet the threat. However, the Cornish army, fearing some trick, stayed where it was. The unfortunate result of this misunderstanding was that the relief force led by Lord Wilmot, comprising only 1700 cavalry and lacking infantry support, faced Waller's army on its own.

Boldly, Wilmot decided to ignore the Roundhead foot and ordered an attack against Waller's cavalry. "No man charged as ours did that day,"

wrote Richard Atkyns who took part in the devastating charge. In spite of brave counter-attacks by Hasilrig and his 'lobsters', the Roundhead cavalry was soon in hurried retreat. All that remained was for the Cornish foot to arrive and finish off the Roundhead foot now left marooned on Roundway down. By evening, Waller's army had ceased to exist.

The supremacy of the Cavalier cavalry had been proved once again.

1643: Desperate Times for Parliament

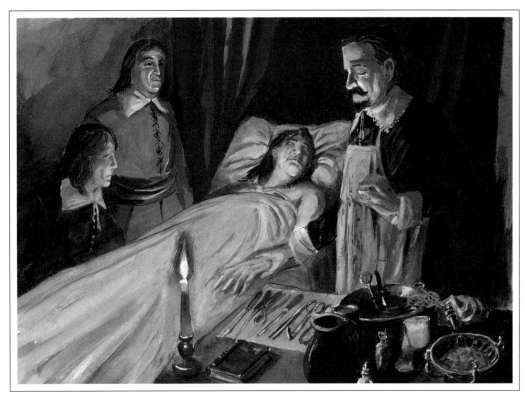

John Hampden, a senior Roundhead commander, was seriously wounded at the battle of Chalgrove. It was he who in 1638 was the King's arch enemy in the Ship Money Trial. It says a lot about the spirit in which the war was fought that the King sent his personal physician to help. It was a humane gesture but to no avail. Hampden died a few days later. It was a great loss to the Parliamentary cause.

The defeat at Roundway Down, following the earlier defeats at Adwalton Moor and at Chalgrove, had left Parliament in a seemingly desperate position. Bristol had been stormed by the Royalists and Gloucester, an important Parliamentary stronghold, was under siege.

However, these defeats and setbacks did not induce despair but seemed to inject a new determination into the Roundhead forces. Matters did not get worse and even took a turn for the better when the Earl of Essex, on his way to relieve Gloucester, had the better of the Cavaliers in a battle at Newbury. News also came of a minor victory at Winceby where a Colonel Oliver Cromwell distinguished himself.

Difficulties for the Roundheads did not lead to a corresponding advantage for the Cavaliers. Although Bristol was a major victory, the King's army had suffered heavy losses in the battle and a serious shortage of manpower effectively prevented them from seizing the initiative.

Both armies suffered from this shortage of manpower. The majority of troops on both sides had to act as guards for key points such as ports, castles and cities, especially those commanding important river crossings.

This meant that the number of soldiers who were able to move about and to attack was only a small percentage of the total strength apparently available. In 1643, the priority on both sides was to create field armies of sufficient strength to strike a decisive blow.

It is well to remember that Scotland was then a separate country, only sharing a King with England and Wales. Many Scottish soldiers had fought as mercenaries on the Continent and were therefore an obvious source of valuable trained men. Shortly before he died in December 1643, John Pym successfully concluded an alliance with the Scots. The 'Committee for the Two Kingdoms' was formed to direct the war effort. The Scots were promised that England would become Presbyterian when victory was won and this would cause problems later. However, the making of this alliance at the end of 1643 undoubtedly changed the balance of power and tilted the war in favour of Parliament and away from the King.

As a direct result of this agreement, in February 1644, a Scottish army of 20,000 men crossed the border and laid siege to Newcastle.

With the Scots now moving into England, the Roundheads marked the change in their fortunes by laying siege to Newark. At first this key Royalist stronghold looked doomed, but the Roundheads had reckoned without Prince Rupert.

Having no doubt of its strategic importance, Rupert hurried from Chester towards Newark collecting what troops he could. He hoped to make up in daring for what he lacked in numbers. So quickly did they move that Sir John Meldrum, the besieging Roundhead's commander, dismissed reports of his approach as fantasy. Rupert's men marched through the moonlit night of March 20/21 to complete their journey.

At dawn he reached Beacon Hill and placed his troops across Meldrum's best line of retreat. Below him he could see the Roundhead besiegers, still blissfully unaware of any danger.

It was vital that the Royalists within Newark helped by attacking at the same time. A message would have to be sent into the city but the problem was to prevent the plans being revealed if it fell into enemy hands. It was therefore reduced to one cryptic sentence: "Let the old drum on the north side be beaten early on the morrow morning." The message was delivered and its meaning understood. The 'old drum' meant Meldrum and they were to sally forth from the North Gate.

The cut-out pieces for this scene are on page 47. The instructions on how to assemble it are inside the back cover.

This area glues to page 29

1644: Newark is Besieged

How to assemble Scene 3
1. Remove page 27 from the book by cutting along the solid line.
2. Cut out the T-shaped piece precisely.
3. Score along the dotted line, creasing firmly to make a valley fold.
4. Check how the grey area on the back of the text fits over this grey
   area so that the flap forms the backdrop of the scene.
   Then glue it carefully into position.

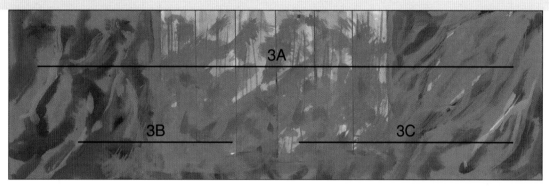

*The attack achieved complete surprise. The
Royalists sallied forth from the North Gate and
overran the fort at Muskham Bridge. At the same
time, under the dynamic leadership of Prince
Rupert, the Cavaliers first routed the Roundhead
cavalry and then pinned Meldrum's bewildered men
against the River Trent. The bridge being lost and
with it their last remaining escape route, Meldrum
offered to surrender. Prince Rupert accepted and
allowed the Roundheads to march away after laying
down their arms. Thirty cannon, four thousand
muskets and a huge supply of powder were taken.*

*Parliament was stunned by the defeat at Newark.
Their frustration was all the greater because they
had just had news of a tremendous Roundhead
victory at Cheriton near Winchester thus effectively
ending the King's hopes of ever taking London.
Although Parliament still had a numerical
supremacy in the North, they needed to find more
capable and resolute leaders if they were to win it.*

1644: The Battle of Marston Moor

In the four months after Newark, the Roundheads and Scots slowly tightened their grip on the King's territories in the north. Newcastle was besieged and then York. Once again the King turned to Prince Rupert to save the situation. Mindful of the defeat at Newark, the Parliamentarians lifted the siege of York and withdrew to Marston Moor, five miles from the city. Rupert was joined there by the Marquis of Newcastle and together they faced the huge combined Parliamentarian force. It was actually made up of three separate armies: the Roundhead Northerners under Sir Thomas Fairfax; the Scots under Lord Leven; and the Army of the Eastern Association led by the Earl of Manchester. The commander of the cavalry's left wing was Lieutenant-General Oliver Cromwell, a Puritan gentleman who had already shown remarkable qualities of leadership and commitment.

Tired from their march on a humid June day, the Royalists made camp. With fading light, they did not expect to fight that day. However, they had miscalculated; a rumbling sound marked the charge of Cromwell's horsemen and the troopers on the Royalist right had barely saddled up when Cromwell's cavalry smashed into them. It was a devastating disciplined charge that sent the Royalists reeling back. Prince Rupert, arriving from the rear, rallied the Cavaliers. "Swounds, do you flee?" he shouted. "Follow me!" A desperate counter-attack checked the leading Roundhead squadrons, but others following behind charged again and sent the Cavaliers flying from the field. For the first time, Parliament had cavalry to match the King's, and in Cromwell the man to lead them.

The quality of Cromwell's troopers, later dubbed 'Ironsides' by Prince Rupert, was shown by the disciplined way in which they quickly re-formed ready for action elsewhere on the battle-field. They were sorely needed, for the battle elsewhere was not going well for the allies. On the far wing, Lord Goring's Cavaliers had proved too strong for the Roundhead horse led by Fairfax, while in the middle the Scottish and Roundhead foot, despite their numerical superiority, were struggling against the Earl of Newcastle's Whitecoats, probably the finest infantry in the King's army. Some Scottish and Roundhead soldiers began to flee the field, among them Lord Leven. For a while it seemed that the whole allied line was in danger of crumbling. However, two Scottish foot regiments gallantly stood their ground against the relentless Royalist attacks and Sir Thomas Fairfax, wounded and cut off from his men, managed to make his way to Cromwell and warn him of the situation.

Cromwell acted decisively and quickly brought his men round behind the Royalist army and charged Goring's hitherto successful cavalry. They broke and fled, leaving their infantry isolated. Seized with renewed heart, the allied foot also advanced and drove the Royalists back. In White Sike Close the Whitecoats faced overwhelming odds and made their last stand. Barely thirty were taken alive. The rest of the Royalist foot fled the field or surrendered.

As darkness fell, the allied soldiers made camp amid the carnage and sang their psalms. Nearly 5,000 men were dead. Hundreds more lay wounded on the field and along the roads leading back to York. The allies had taken 1,500 prisoners. It was a decisive victory for Parliament and the King's northern army had ceased to exist.

The Roundhead cavalry under Cromwell and Fairfax turn the tide of battle and ensure a decisive victory for Parliament at Marston Moor.

1644/1645: Frustration Sets in

The great success at Marston Moor in July 1644, offered Parliament and their Scottish allies the prospect of total victory. It was, however, an opportunity that was squandered. Although most of the Royalist north did come under Parliamentary control, the next few months would show that the Parliamentary leadership lacked the skill and vision to win the war.

In June, Waller had suffered a humiliating defeat by the King at Cropredy Bridge. In September, Essex's army had been trapped in Cornwall and forced to surrender. In October, Parliament finally managed to combine its armies and confront the King, only to suffer a humiliating defeat at the Second Battle of Newbury.

With such a string of defeats and also serious disagreements within the high command, the demoralised Roundhead armies suffered mutinies and desertions and began to fall apart. To the frustration of Parliament and all involved, an end to the war seemed further away than ever.

Inevitably this frustration led to recrimination. Cromwell openly criticised his commander, the Earl of Manchester, for incompetence and defeatism.

The Puritans became increasingly divided, with the English and Scottish Presbyterians wanting to make peace with the King, if only he would agree to the Church of England becoming Presbyterian. A more radical group of Puritans called the Independents, and including Cromwell, wanted more religious toleration for all Protestants and the total defeat of the King.

"If we fight a hundred times and beat him ninety nine, he will still be King," lamented Manchester. "But if he beat us but once, we shall be hanged."

"My Lord," replied Cromwell, "if this be so, why did we take up arms at first?"

On December 9, 1644 Cromwell, in an apparent attempt to defuse the situation, suggested that members of both Houses of Parliament should not also hold commissions in the army. "I hope we have such true English hearts and zealous affections towards the general weal (good) of our mother country, as no members of either House will scruple to deny themselves and their private interests for the public good."

This meant, in effect, that Essex, Waller and Manchester would all resign their commands. It would also apply to Cromwell himself. The House of Commons readily agreed to this 'Self-denying Ordinance', as it was called. It was also accepted by the Lords once further peace negotiations with the King had failed. The main commanders then all stood down. This action cleared the way for the creation of a national army, led by professional officers and paid directly by Parliament. It would also be an army committed to total victory.

In the spring of 1645 the 'The New Model Army' was formed out of the remains of Waller's, Essex's and Manchester's regiments. The cavalry, moulded by Cromwell, was already a formidable force, but in the early months the infantry was far inferior to that of the Royalists. Overall command was given to Sir Thomas Fairfax, and command of the foot to Sir Philip Skippon. No cavalry commander was appointed, because apart from Cromwell there was no suitable candidate.

After four years of an increasingly savage war, disenchanted citizens now attacked Roundhead and Cavalier alike. Robber bands roamed the countryside. Though both sides were grimly optimistic, there was a growing realisation that another year of stalemate would see the country slide ever deeper into chaos.

Something had to be done and in spite of the Self-denying Ordinance, Cromwell was appointed commander of the cavalry.

More than fifty copies of this famous miniature portrait of Cromwell, 'Warts and All' by Samuel Cooper were made in his studio and were widely distributed. Most have since disappeared. Cromwell's contribution to victory at Naseby and to the development of The New Model Army was to prove crucial.

1645: The Battle of Naseby

Fairfax himself was able to capture a royal standard, but it was Cromwell and his 'Ironsides' who once again were the decisive factor in the Roundhead victory.

The village of Naseby is in Leicestershire and it was here on June 14, 1645 that the New Model Army first demonstrated its total supremacy over the Royalists. Not only did it have superiority in numbers of two-to-one but the cavalry was far better disciplined. Thomas Fairfax was in command and showed great verve and bravery. Although his helmet had been lost in an earlier mêlée, he hurled himself into the heart of the fighting and personally captured a royal standard.

However, once again it was Cromwell who led the decisive cavalry charge. His disciplined and well-trained 'Ironsides' re-formed and were ready for further action whilst the Cavaliers charged off the battlefield. By one o'clock in the afternoon, the only Cavaliers remaining on the field were either wounded or prisoners. It was such a decisive victory for Cromwell and the Roundheads that from this date it was clear that the war was won, even though it was not yet over.

1646: The War Comes to an End

Apart from the victory on the battlefield, Naseby also provided some dramatic evidence which further turned public opinion against the King. In the captured Royalist baggage train were letters that Charles had written to his wife over the past two years. They proved beyond question that he was planning to bring an army of the hated Irish Catholics to England. The publication of 'The King's Cabinet Opened' was a devastating blow to the Royalist cause.

During the following months, the New Model Army proceeded to retake, one by one, the remaining Royalist strongholds. On September 10, Prince Rupert surrendered Bristol to Sir Thomas Fairfax. Although his nephew was undoubtedly one of his ablest generals, Charles stripped him of his command and ordered him to leave the country.

In early October, Cromwell, having taken Winchester, arrived before Basing House which had been besieged since August 1643. John Paulet, fifth Marquis of Winchester, had turned his house into a fortress and vowed never to surrender. Inside were known Catholics. To the Roundhead chaplains in the New Model Army this was a 'nest of idolatry'. A week's bombardment was followed by an assault and Basing House fell. On Cromwell's orders it was destroyed.

Oxford was besieged and fell in June 1646 but Charles had escaped and made his way to the Scottish army at Newark. Nine months of negotiations with the Scots followed but Charles refused to accept a Presbyterian Church in England and agreement could not be reached. Frustrated, the Scots handed the King over to Parliament and went home. Although Charles was a prisoner at Holdenby House in Northamptonshire, he enjoyed a gracious custody. He could play chess and bowls and was allowed to walk in the gardens but could not leave. His policy for the next two years was to talk to his enemies but never to come to an agreement. By this strategy he hoped he could exploit the growing differences among the various Parliamentary factions.

The Civil War had unleashed great passions and great misery. It had also caused men and women to think about what was wrong with their world. Portable printing presses meant that a flood of pamphlets was being produced by both Royalists and Parliamentarians even as the war was going on. After the Roundhead victory, despite orders for all publications to be licensed, the flood continued. Many in the provinces were unhappy at the high taxation which the costs of the war had demanded and they resented the power of the new men running the county committees. The desire for some kind of settlement was strong. The difficulty was to decide if any settlement should aim to re-establish traditional ways or to seek to build a new and more godly world?

Religion remained at the heart of the debate. The Church of England was dismantled and the frail Archbishop of Canterbury, William Laud, was finally taken from the Tower to the block in 1645. In June 1646, Parliament endorsed a Presbyterian form of worship, but it was neither completely like the Scottish Kirk nor was it acceptable to the radical Puritans, the Independents.

The Independents had gained a foothold in the New Model Army, where fiery chaplains such as Hugh Peter preached to the soldiers. By 1647, 'Leveller' ideas were also being actively discussed. Levellers believed that there should be more justice and liberty even for those who did not belong to the ruling classes. They thought that the soldiers had fought for a cause: that freedom of worship should be allowed and that more men should be given the vote. 'Freeborn' John Lilburne, who at eighteen had been whipped through the streets for his opposition to Charles's bishops, was determined that the end of the war would not just bring about the restoration of the pre-war world. As he told the House of Lords, "All you intended when you set us a-fighting was merely to unhorse our old riders and tyrants that you might get up and ride us in their stead." It is not surprising that his ideas, together with those of other leveller writers, helped to push the army into mutiny in May 1647.

The immediate cause was pay. Increasingly worried at the political and religious militancy of the New Model Army, on May 25, 1646 the House of Commons voted for the immediate disbandment of the infantry. They offered only eight week's back pay even though the foot soldiers were eighteen weeks in arrears and the cavalry forty-three. Refusing to disband, the army set up its headquarters at Newmarket. On June 3, a junior officer, Cornet Joyce, arrived at Holdenby House with a troop of cavalry to take the King away. When asked by the King what commission he had to seize his person, Joyce turned and pointed to his troops. The King agreed to go with them.

Meanwhile, an Army Council had been established and on June 14 the army issued its first political programme. They declared "We were not a mere mercenary army, hired to serve any arbitrary power of a state, but called forth to the defence of our own and the people's just rights and liberties."

King Charles had by now met Cromwell for the first time, as well as Cromwell's stern Puritan son-in-law Henry Ireton. It was Ireton who had written peace terms, called 'The Heads of the Proposals'. These would have kept the King and the ruling classes in power. However, Charles would not agree to such a settlement. In August the New Model Army lost patience and marched to take London. The King was moved to Hampton Court and in October the Army Council sat down in a church at Putney to discuss new proposals called 'The Agreement of the People'. Cromwell, who was chairman, commented: "Truly this paper does contain in it very great alterations of the very government of the kingdom."

Basing House had been besieged since August 1643, but in October 1645 after a week's bombardment, it fell to an assault by the New Model Army.

1648: Negotiations Fail and War is Resumed

The Army Council included generals who were known as the 'grandees' and representatives from each regiment who were known as the 'agitators'. Agreement proved to be impossible. The agitators argued for reforms to help the poor and allow them some say in government while the grandees, despite having fought the King, supported a more traditional government. During this power struggle the determination of the grandees to maintain military discipline and obedience whatever the cost was clearly shown. On November 15, at Corkbush Field near Ware a mutiny was put down, the ringleaders arrested and one Richard Arnold was shot.

By then, however, the first steps towards a resumption of the civil war had already taken place. On November 11, 1647, Charles had slipped away from Hampton Court with surprising ease and travelled south west to the Isle of Wight. He gave himself into the custody of Colonel Hammond, the governor of the island. In Carisbrooke Castle on Boxing Day he signed an 'Engagement' with the Scots that in return for the military help of a Scottish army he would make England Presbyterian for a trial period of three years. He also tried to escape from the castle. He had the help of a laundry woman's maid, but became stuck fast in the window of his bedchamber.

The summer of 1648 was the worst in living memory. Daily, it seemed, cold wind and rain lashed the country. Rivers burst their banks and roads remained winter quagmires. Parliament called for a national day of fasting and prayer that the country might atone for its evident sins. It was certainly not the sort of weather in which to conduct war. Risings in Kent, Essex and South Wales were as much to do with the unpopularity of the high taxation and the Puritan county committees as support for the King. They and the more specifically Royalist risings were put down by different New Model regiments.

The King's best hope of improving the situation lay with the Scottish Marquis of Hamilton, now struggling southwards along the muddy lanes of north Lancashire. He was to be joined by another Royalist army under Sir Marmaduke Langdale but, on August 17, Cromwell with 9,000 soldiers, mainly of units of the New Model Army, launched a devastating attack on them before they could meet up with Hamilton. The Roundheads then swept on to secure Preston and the vital bridges over the River Ribble, thus cutting Hamilton's men off from Scotland. Nightfall brought a brief respite but the next day, as they tried to retreat southwards, they found themselves in growing disarray with Cromwell's troopers hard at their heels. Over the following two days, Hamilton's army was systematically destroyed. The last remnant surrendered at Warrington and Hamilton himself was captured at Uttoxeter.

The Second Civil War was effectively over.

At the end of 1647, the Scots withdrew support for Parliament and made a new agreement to support the King. Fighting broke out again but this second phase of the civil war was decisively brought to an end at the battle of Preston when Cromwell defeated the Scottish army under the Marquis of Hamilton.

1649: Charles is Brought to Trial

Charles took his seat, an impassive figure dressed in black, with the silver star of the Order of the Garter on his cloak. Around his neck was a jewel containing a picture of his wife.

After the battle of Preston, the last Royalist strongholds surrendered. Parliament resumed negotiations with Charles at Newport but again no settlement could be agreed. Another year of fighting had exhausted the patience of the army and many felt that Charles had forfeited his right to be King. In November the army sent a 'remonstrance' to Parliament demanding his punishment. To the militants he was 'that grand and capital author of all our woes.' When Parliament refused to discuss the remonstrance and also continued the Newport talks, the Council of Officers took drastic action. At 7.00 am on December 6, 1648 Colonel Pride and 1,000 troopers prevented those MP's who had voted to continue negotiations with the King from entering the Commons. The militants now controlled the 'Rump', the name given to the reduced membership of what was left of the Long Parliament. The Rump now passed an ordinance creating a special High Court to try the King.

At 2.30 on the afternoon of January 20, 1649, Charles Stuart, King of England, entered the court. The chosen venue was the Great Hall of Westminster and a crowd had packed into the vast building for, as Thomas Harrison, one of those who was to sign the death warrant, later wrote: "It was not a thing done in a corner." This was to be a public trial.

From behind the red baize-covered bench that faced him, the president of the Court, John Bradshaw, wearing a hat reinforced with steel for extra protection, explained that the court had been constituted by Parliament according to the power and trust reposed in it by the People. The prosecutor, John Cook, then read the charge. Charles was accused of high treason, in that he had "traitorously and maliciously levied war against the present Parliament and the People therein represented." He was attacked as a tyrant, a traitor, a murderer and a public and an implacable enemy of the Commonwealth of England.

Charles's response was calm and was delivered without his usual stammer. He refused to plead either "guilty" or "not guilty" but asked "I would know by what power I am called hither." When Bradshaw replied that it was by the authority of the Commons of England, the King denied the right of any court to try him.

Over the next few days, Bradshaw and Cook tried to continue, but without success, as Charles persisted in denying the legality of the court. Eventually he was led away and the trial proceeded without him in the painted chamber at Westminster.

On Saturday January 27, the King was brought back into the Great Hall to hear the inevitable sentence:

"For all which treasons and crimes this court doth adjudge that the said Charles Stuart, as a tyrant, traitor, murderer and public enemy to the good people of this nation, shall be put to death by the severing of his head from his body."

Charles tried to address the court but was hurried away by the guards. Oliver Cromwell made sure that a sufficient number of Parliamentarians signed the death warrant and thus became joint regicides.

The execution took place on Tuesday January 30. The day before, Charles had said goodbye to his younger children. He rose early on the fateful morning, asking for two shirts because in the bitter cold, he did not want his shivers to be seen as fear.

A large crowd had gathered in Whitehall. Against the banqueting hall, a scaffold, draped in black, had been erected level with the first floor windows. The crowd waited, cold but patient. Between them and the scaffold were ranks of soldiers. At two o'clock, Charles emerged on to the scaffold from a window, enlarged to become a makeshift door, with Bishop Juxon at his side.

The cut-out pieces for this scene are on page 47. The instructions on how to assemble it are inside the back cover.

This area glues to page 41.

1649: The Execution

How to assemble Scene 4
1. Remove page 39 from the book by cutting along the solid line.
2. Cut out the T-shaped piece precisely.
3. Score along the dotted line, creasing firmly to make a valley fold.
4. Check how the grey area on the back of the text fits over this grey area so that the flap forms the backdrop of the scene. Then glue it carefully into position.

4A

4B

4C

As was usual at executions the King was allowed to speak. "I never did begin a war with the two houses of Parliament," he began. He then said that he desired the liberty and freedom of his people as much as anybody, and proclaimed that he died a Christian of the Church of England. Finally he put on a white satin cap to keep his hair in place and lowered himself to the block, disappearing from the view of the people. His last word was "Remember."

The axe fell, the executioner held up the severed head and the crowd groaned. Some moved to dip their handkerchiefs in the King's blood but most went quietly away.

Charles's head was to be sewn back on the next day. His body was embalmed and then taken to St. George's Chapel at Windsor to be interred on February 9. On his coffin it said simply 'King Charles' and the date.

1649: The Commonwealth is Established

Cromwell took decisive action to end the deadlock in Parliament. Seizing the Mace, he said "What shall we do with this bauble? Here take it away" The following day someone put a notice on the door: "This House to Let."

Between 1649 and 1660 the government of England was Republican. Both the Monarchy and the House of Lords were abolished shortly after the execution and the republic established as the Commonwealth. There was no Head of State and power was uneasily shared by a Council, the Rump, and The New Model Army.

By 1650 Oliver Cromwell had subdued the Irish, who had been in rebellion since 1641. Most of the garrisons of Drogheda and Wexford were put to the sword. He returned to England to become captain-general (commander-in-chief) of the army, Fairfax being unwilling to lead the next campaign into Scotland. There were many people, especially in Scotland, who thought that at the moment the axe fell, Charles's eldest son Charles became King Charles II of England and Scotland. The Scots, still wishing to make England Presbyterian, then made an alliance with the new King and prepared for war. However Cromwell and the New Model Army were equal to the task and on September 3, 1650 they won a major victory at Dunbar, east of Edinburgh. "The Lord hath done this," wrote an elated Cromwell.

Gathering yet more troops, Charles II marched south into England at the head of a Scottish army. Cromwell allowed them to pass and then inflicted a major defeat at Worcester which finally brought the civil wars to an end. After this defeat, the young claimant to the throne managed to reach Brighton and escape to France. A price of £1,000 was placed on his head and a description circulated of a tall dark man "upwards of two yards high."

The Royalist cause was now effectively dead, but the Commonwealth did not flourish. The leveller proposals had failed by 1649 and John Lilburne, although acquitted of high treason by a London jury, was banished by the Rump in 1651. The Independents within the New Model Army were increasingly unhappy by the lack of Parliamentary reforms. On April 23, 1653 Cromwell took decisive action. Posting musketeers at the doors of the House of Commons he entered Parliament and condemned the actions of the Rump. "Come, come, I will put an end to your prating." He summoned his musketeers and ordered them to turn out the MP's. The following day someone put a notice on the door: "This House to Let."

By the end of the year, the Commonwealth had been ended. Cromwell, sadly accepting the failure of an experimental Parliament, became Lord Protector on December 16, 1653.

Thus the second stage of the Republic began.

1653: The Protectorate

Oliver Cromwell was to govern Britain as protector and captain-general of the army until his death on September 3, 1658. During that time he tried to heal the wounds of the civil wars and to govern fairly and evenly but he was never able to balance successfully the claims of Parliament and the power of the New Model Army. The army had become one of the most effective forces in Europe and were admired for their success abroad. However, most people resented the continuing high taxes and the determination of the Independents to bring about a strict and godly reformation of manners and morals from which no-one could escape. The peak of unpopularity came in 1655, when the Country came under the direct rule of the army and was administered by Major-Generals. Some of these army officers created a 'spoil-sport' impression by closing down alehouses, horse-race meetings and theatres. Decorative features in churches were vandalised and even the Maypole was banned.

Cromwell, still desperately seeking a settlement, accepted that this experiment had failed and sought to return the government to a more traditional Parliament of two houses. In 1657, Parliament offered him the Crown, but after deep consideration, he decided not to accept, probably because of army opposition. He was re-installed as Protector on June 26, 1657 but only lived for a further fourteen months.

"I desire that you use all your skill to paint my picture truly like me and not to flatter me at all; but remark all these roughnesses, pimples, warts and everything, other I never will pay a farthing for it."

Such were Cromwell's carefully recorded instructions to the artist Peter Lely.

1660: The Restoration of the Monarchy

On May 25, 1660 Charles returned to England. As he landed on the beach at Dover, he was met by General Monck. The general surrendered his sword to the King, symbolically placing the army and the nation into his care.

It is remarkable that less than two years after the death of Cromwell, the Stuart heir, Charles II should be welcomed back as King. But that is what happened. The Republic had staggered towards collapse, becoming probably one of the most unpopular governments the country has ever had. Oliver's son, Richard Cromwell, was appointed Protector on his father's death but lacked his father's skills and retired after only four months. The army and Parliament then struggled for power until, early in 1660, General Monck marched south from Scotland to take over London. Skillfully, he turned the clock back. He recalled the Long Parliament and persuaded them to dissolve themselves. New elections were held in the spring and it was this 'Convention Parliament' which invited Charles I's son back to his kingdom. Returning in the flagship once called 'Naseby' but now re-christened 'Royal Charles', the new King arrived in London on his thirtieth birthday to cheers, bells and posies of flowers.

Most of the former Roundheads were pardoned, although not all. Thirteen suffered execution for their part in the civil wars and the Republic. Cromwell's body was dug up, hanged at Tyburn and his head displayed on a pike on Westminster Bridge. The New Model Army was disbanded.

Charles II was to die in his bed in February 1685 after a colourful reign of twenty five years. He had been able to manage the continuing problems of religion, finance and Parliament and to keep his throne. His brother and successor, James II, was less successful at maintaining the balance between conflicting demands. He had become a Catholic and this decision, together with the ambitions of his son-in-law William of Orange, led eventually to the 'Glorious Revolution' of 1688/89. James was forced to flee and William and his wife Mary, James's daughter, became joint monarchs.

Gradually many of the issues of the Civil War were resolved and by the eighteenth century it was clear that, in the struggle between King and Parliament, Parliament was the final victor.

♣ 1G

♣ 1H

♣ 1F

♣ 1E

1B

1C

1D

1A

1G

1H

♣ 2E

♣ 2D

♣ 2F

2A

2B

2C

2E

2F

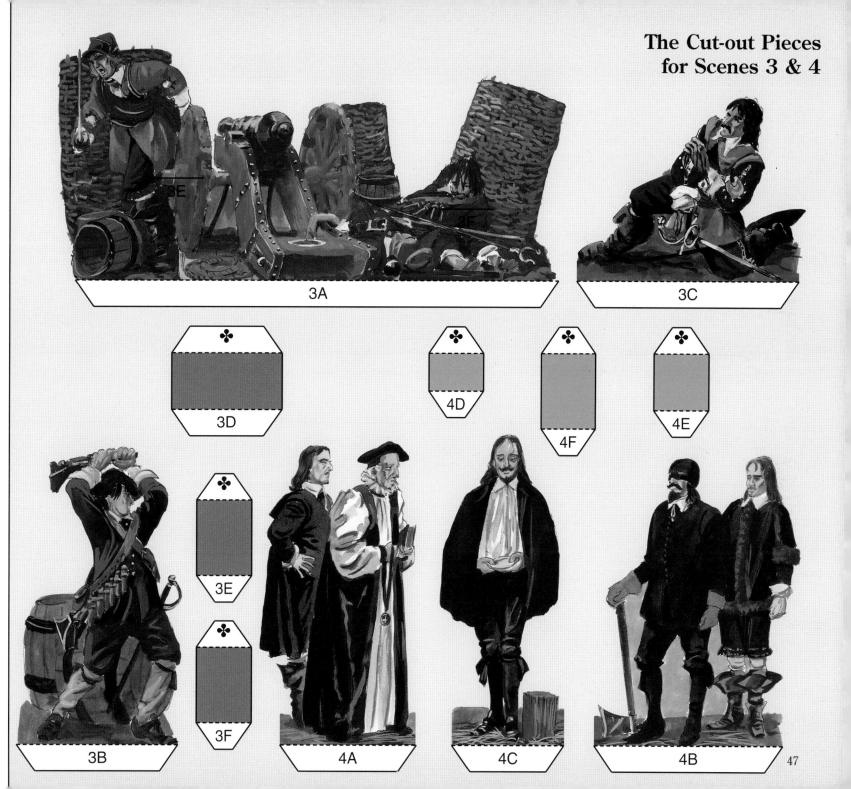

The Cut-out Pieces
for Scenes 3 & 4

3A

3C

3D

4D

4F

4E

3E

3E

3B

3F

4A

4C

4B

47